BAKER ELEMENTARY SCHOOL

Energy

How You Use Different Forms of Energy

DEVELOPED IN COOPERATION WITH FERNBANK MUSEUM OF NATURAL HISTORY ATLANTA, GEORGIA

No part of this publication may be reproduced in whole or in part, or stored in a retrieval system, or transmitted in any form or by any means, electronic, mechanical, photocopying, recording, or otherwise, without written permission of the publisher. For information regarding permission, write to Scholastic Inc., Instructional Publishing Group, 730 Broadway, New York, N.Y. 10003

Copyright © 1993 by Scholastic Inc. All rights reserved. Published by Scholastic Inc. Printed in the U.S.A.
ISBN 0-590-26142-8
2 3 4 5 6 7 8 9 10 09 99 98 97 96 95 94 93 92

THE PHYSICAL WORLD IS GOVERNED BY THE PROPERTIES AND INTERACTIONS OF MATTER AND ENERGY.

Energy

Energy exists in different forms.

Read-Aloud

Energy

Light, heat, sound, and electricity are different forms of energy.

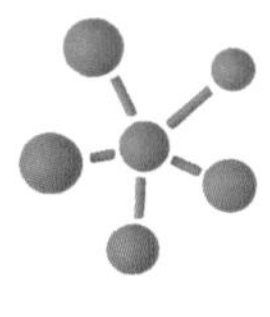

Energy moves and changes matter.

SIMPLE SCIENCE SAYS: Take One Mirror
by Melvin Berger
Literature

There are renewable and nonrenewable sources of energy.

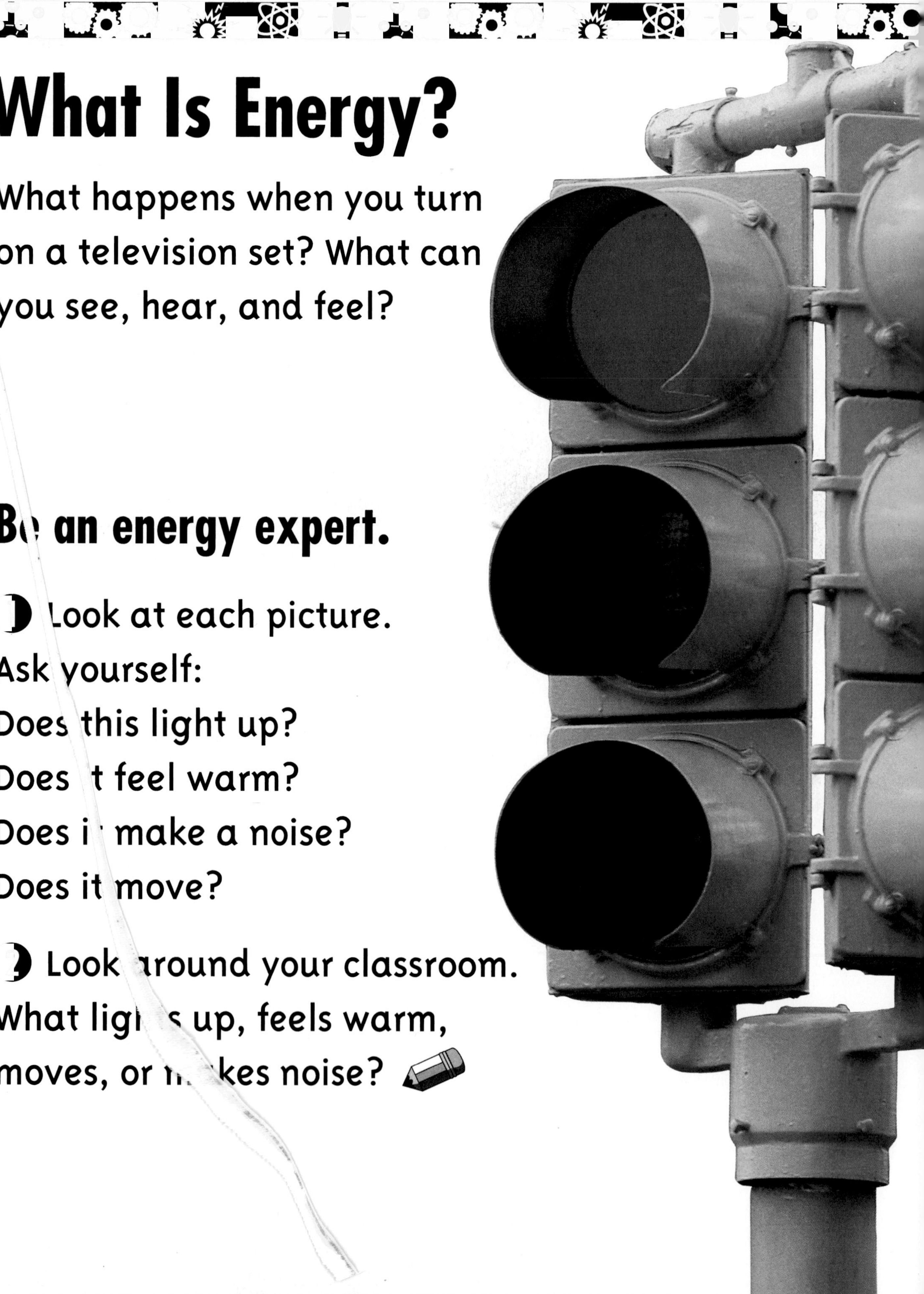

What Is Energy?

What happens when you turn on a television set? What can you see, hear, and feel?

Be an energy expert.

1. Look at each picture.
Ask yourself:
Does this light up?
Does it feel warm?
Does it make a noise?
Does it move?

2. Look around your classroom.
What lights up, feels warm, moves, or makes noise?

Energy moves. Energy also moves and changes other things. Light, heat, sound, and electricity are some forms of energy.

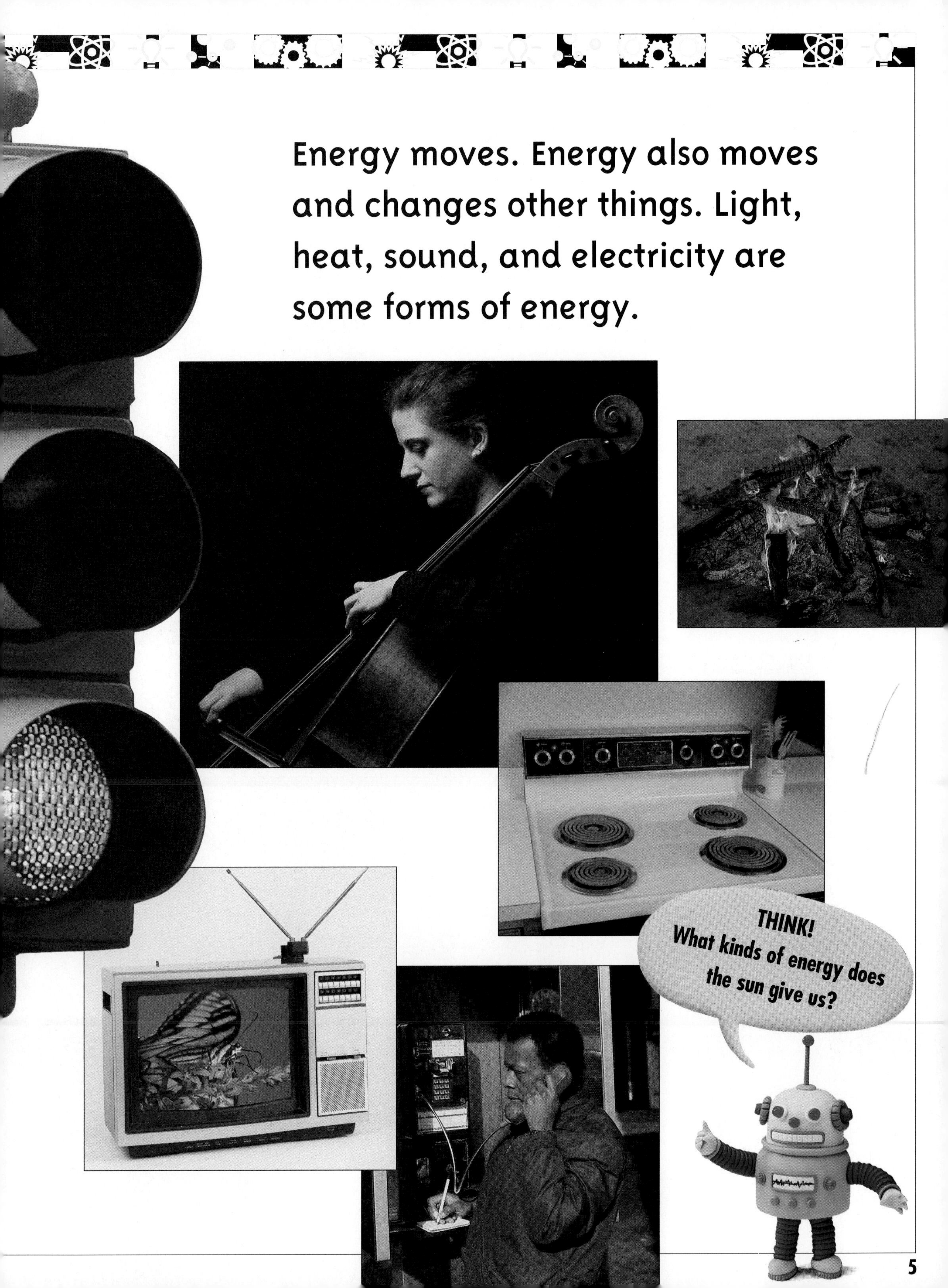

What Is Light Energy?

Light is a form of energy that you can see. You can see it in a television, you can see it in a streetlight. What else gives off light?

How can light energy change things?

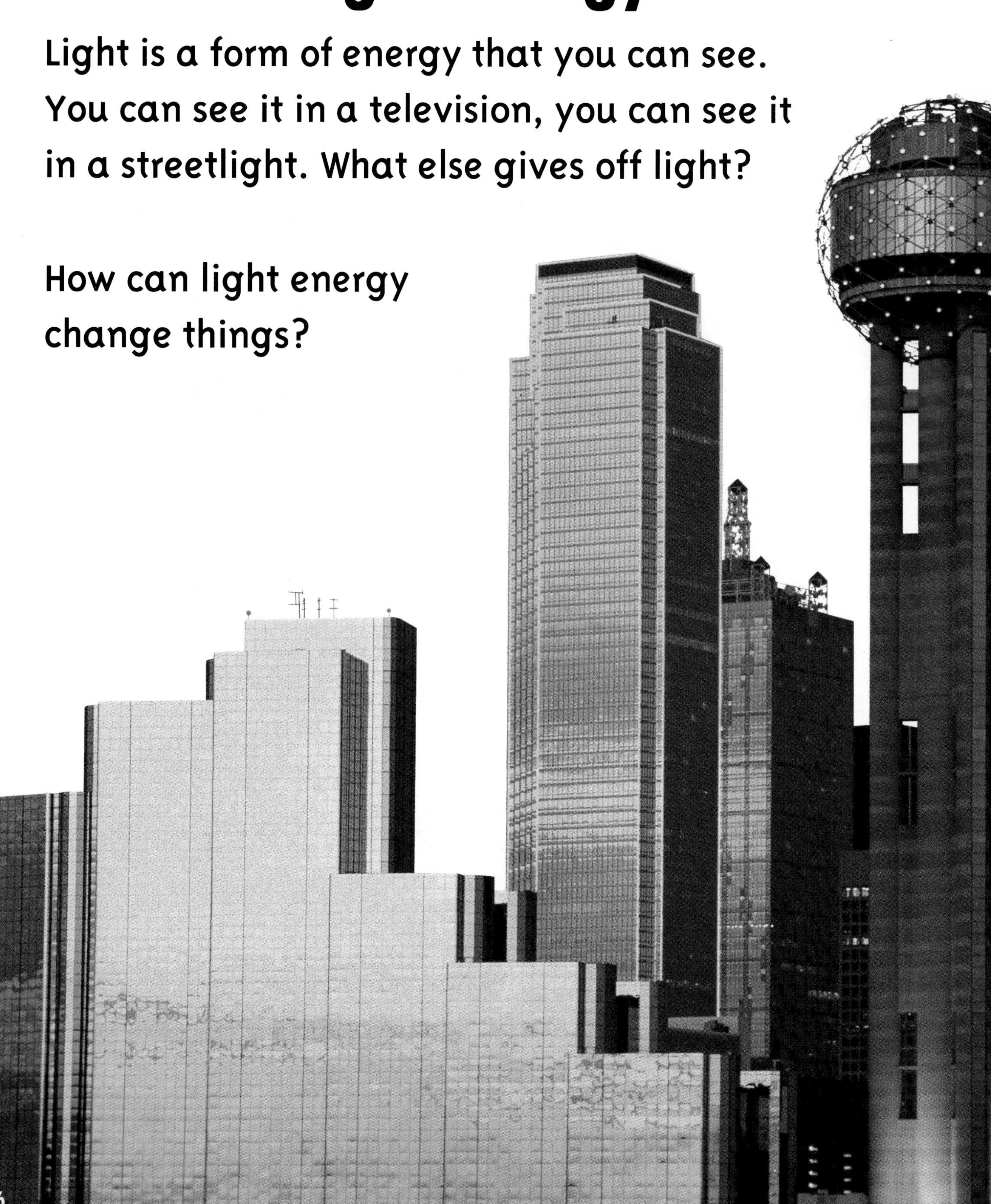

Make a sun picture.

❶ Cut the blue paper in half. Cut a shape from one half. Tape that half to a sunny window. Tape the solid half over it.

❷ After two days, take down both halves. What do you see?

How Does Light Energy Move?

Light comes from many sources.
But how does it move?

Put on a shadow show.

You need:
Light
White paper or white sheet

❶ Set up your shadow screen using white paper.

❷ Using your hands and a flashlight, make up some shadow animals for your classmates. What happens when the beam of light hits your hands?

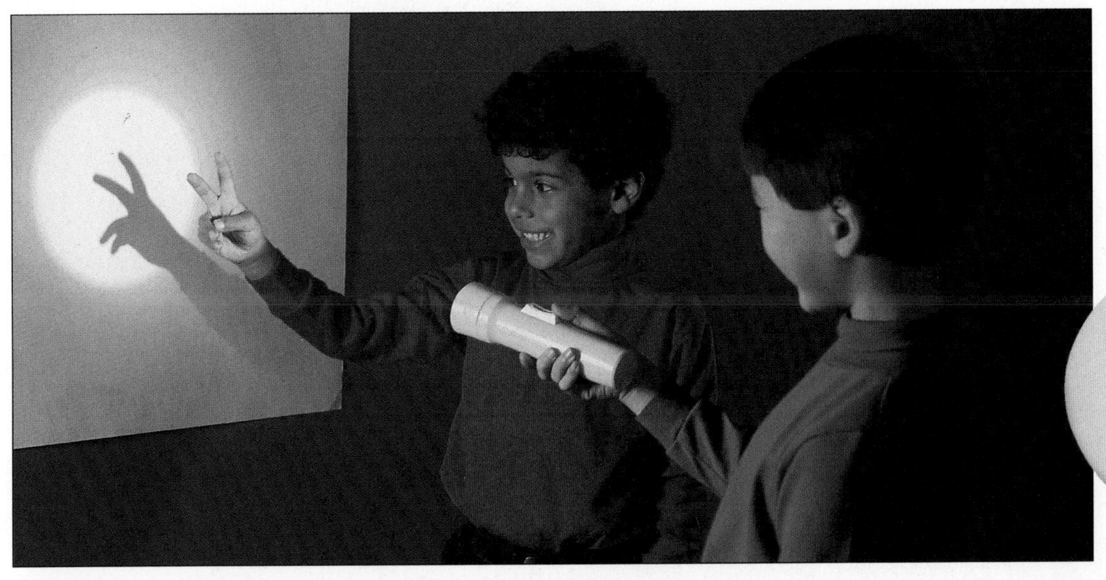

Light travels in a straight line. When it hits something, it either passes through or bounces off.

How Can You Control Light?

You saw that light travels in a straight line and that it bounces, or reflects. How can you make light go where you want it to go?

You need:
Mirrors

Move a light beam.

❶ Put your mirror in the light and move it around slowly, then quickly. What do you see?

❷ Now work with a partner to reflect light from each other's mirror. Where does the light end up? Can you stop the light?

THINK!
How can you control the light from a light bulb?

What Is Heat Energy?

If you stand in the sunlight, how does your skin feel? The sun gives off light energy. It also gives off heat energy. What are some other sources of heat? Can heat change things?

Brew some tea.

You need:
- Water
- Two cups
- Herbal tea bags
- Masking tape
- Markers

1. Label the cups. Fill one cup with cold water and one with hot water. Put a tea bag in each cup and watch them for a minute. What happens?

2. Check the cups again in two minutes. How does the tea look in each cup? What happened?

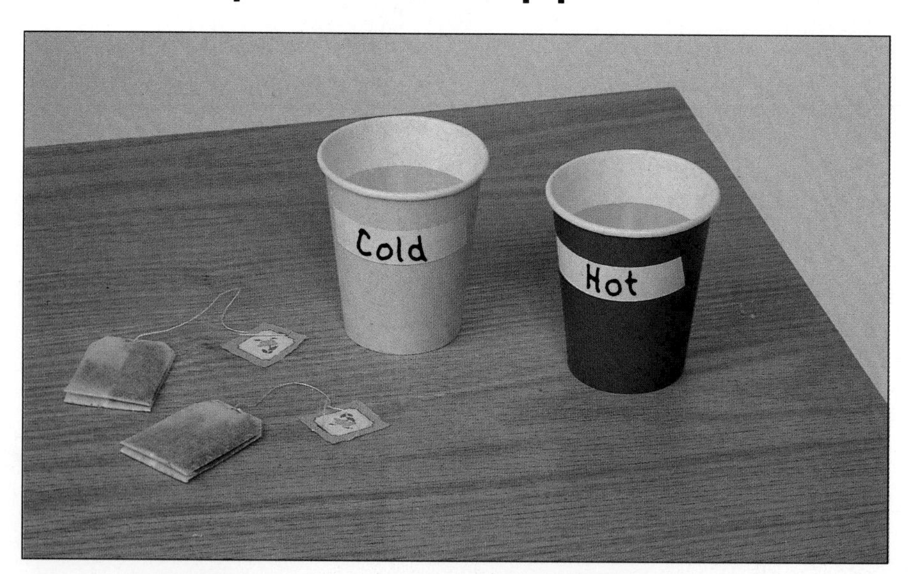

Where is heat coming from in this picture? How is heat changing the pan and the batter?

How Does Heat Energy Move?

What feels warm? What feels cold?
How does something cold get warm?

Move some heat.

1 Put hot water in the pan and cold water in the cup. Put a thermometer in each and read them.

2 Now put the cup of cold water in the pan. Wait 15 minutes and check the water temperatures again. What happened?

Heat travels from warm objects to colder ones. What changes is heat causing here?

How Can You Control Heat?

Heat will move from warmer to cooler objects. How do people get and keep heat where they want it?

Save heat.

1 Think about how you might keep a cup of water warm in a box. Then use any or all of the materials to build a heat saver.

You need:
- Markers or crayons
- Box with lid
- Cups
- Foil
- Newspaper
- Fabric scraps
- Plastic bags
- Thermometers

2 Now put one cup of hot water on the table and another in your heat saver. Check the temperatures.

3 After 15 minutes, check the temperatures of both cups of water. Which water cools off first? Why?

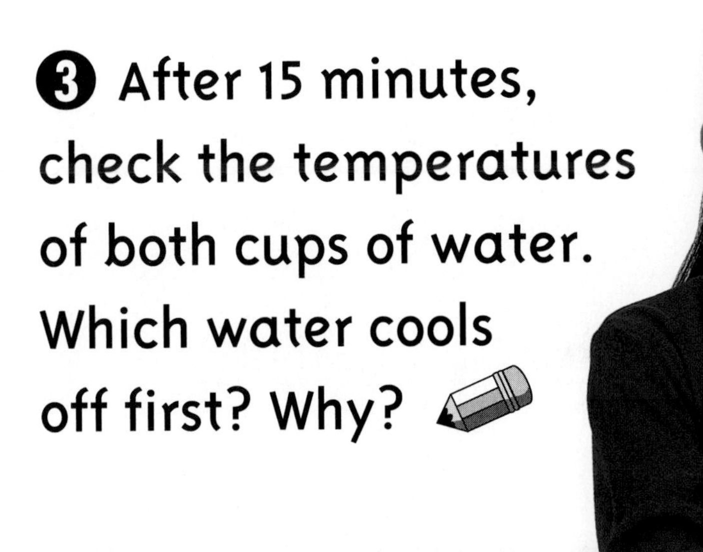

THINK!
What objects work like your heat saver?

What Is Sound Energy?

Like light and heat, sound is a form of energy. Sit quietly for a few minutes. Listen. What sounds do you hear? Do these pictures give you any sound ideas? What sounds can you make?

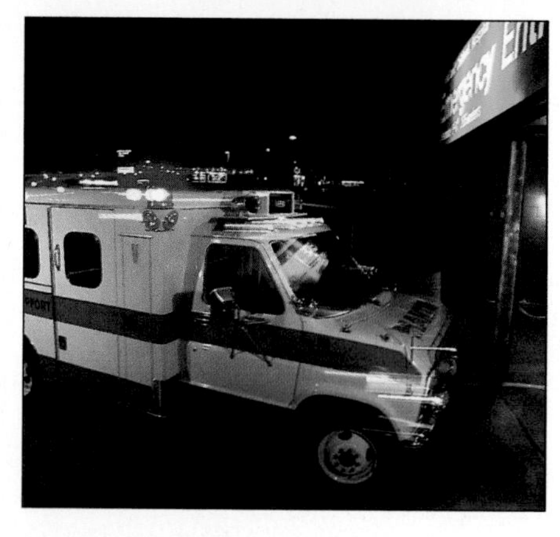

Be a sound maker.

❶ Feel your throat while you sing. What do you feel?

❷ Hold a ruler on the edge of your desk. Pluck the end. What do you hear and see? Pluck the ruler over your knee. What happens now?

Sound is made when objects move back and forth very quickly, or vibrate. Hard objects make more sound than soft ones because they vibrate more.

How Does Sound Energy Move?

Sound is all around you. How does it reach your ears?

Tap into sound.

You need:
Tuning fork
Pan
Water

❶ Put water in a pan. Gently dip the tuning fork into the water. What happens?

❷ Tap the tuning fork against your desk. Touch it lightly. What do you feel? Tap it again and put it in the water. What happens?

Just as waves travel through water, sound waves travel through the air to your ears.

How is sound traveling between these two children?

How Can You Control Sound?

Sounds can be loud or soft. You can change the loudness on a television. How else can you control sound?

You need:
Plastic straw
Scissors
Ruler

Tune a straw.

❶ Cut one end of your straw into a V-shape. Then blow on the V-end. What happens?

❷ Cut three centimeters off the other end. Blow again. What happens?

❸ Cut off some more and blow again. What do you notice now?

How is this person controlling sound?

THINK!
Why do people need to know how to control sound?

What Is Electrical Energy?

Have you ever heard thunder? How does it sound? What other energy is at work in a storm?

Like light, heat, and sound, electrical energy is found in nature.

Find electrical energy.

❶ Blow up your balloon and tie the end with string.

❷ Rub the balloon with wool, then touch the balloon. What happens?

❸ Tape the string to a table. Rub the balloon again, then hold the palm of your hand over it. What happens?

How Do People Use Electrical Energy?

People put electrical energy to work as electricity. How do they control electricity?

You need:
- Battery
- Wires
- Bulb
- Masking tape

Make the connection.

❶ Use the materials you have to light the bulb.

❷ Now how can you turn off the light?

Electricity travels through metal wires in a loop or circuit. Most of the electricity you use comes from factories called power plants.

What other energy forms do these machines change electricity to? What other machines use electricity?

THINK!
Why should you save electricity?

Where Do People Get Electricity?

Some of the light, heat, and sound energy you use comes from electricity. How is all that electricity made?

Some power plants use fuels from inside the earth to make electricity.

Will there always be enough of these resources to make enough electricity? What else can people use?

The wind can run machines that make electricity.

Special panels can change sunlight into electricity.

The power of moving water can be used, too.

How Much Energy Do You Need?

Look at the picture. What kinds of energy does it take to make a TV show? Where does the energy come from?

Lights! Camera! Action!

❶ Write a short TV script about using and saving energy.

❷ Work in small groups to decide which roles you will play, and present your show to your class.

What other ways did your class think of to save energy? How can you save energy?

Beam: A beam is a straight line of light. Electric lights, campfires, and the sun all send out beams of light.

Electricity: Electricity, or electrical energy, is a kind of energy that a battery can hold and a wire can carry. People use electricity to run certain machines.

Energy: Energy is the ability to make things move and change. Light, heat, sound, and electricity are forms of energy.

Heat: Heat is the kind of energy you can feel as warmth.

Light: Light is the kind of energy your eyes can see.

Reflect: When an object bounces light or sound energy in a new direction, the object is reflecting that form of energy.